The Adventures of Sally Elephant Who Likes Being Upside Down

Michael P. Watts

Copyright © 2020 by Michael Watts.

ISBN-978-1-6455-0858-8

COVER ARTWORK:
Michael Parekowhai
Ngati Whakarongo
New Zealand b.1968
The World Turns 2011-12
Bronze
488 x 456 x 293cm (approx.)
Commissioned 2011 to mark the fifth anniversary of the opening of the Gallery of Modern Art in 2006 and 20 years of the Asia Pacific Triennial of Contemporary Art. This project has received financial assistance from the Queensland Government through art+place Queensland Public Art Fund and from the Queensland Art Gallery Foundation
Collection: Queensland Art Gallery | Gallery of Modern Art
Photograph: Michael Watts

All rights reserved. No part of this book may be used or reproduced by any means, graphic, electronic, or mechanical, including photocopying, recording, taping or by any information storage retrieval system without the written permission of the author except in the case of brief quotations embodied in critical articles and reviews.

This is a work of fiction. All of the characters, names, incidents, organizations, and dialogue in this novel are either the products of the author's imagination or are used fictitiously.

All rights reserved. No part of this book may be reproduced or transmitted in any form or by any means, electronic or mechanical, including photocopying, recording, or by any information storage and retrieval system, without permission in writing from the copyright owner.

The views expressed in this work are solely those of the author and do not necessarily reflect the views of the publisher, and the publisher hereby disclaims any responsibility for them.

Matchstick Literary
1-888-306-8885
orders@matchliterary.com

CONTENTS

Acknowledgements vii
1   Where it all began 1
2   The nickname 3
3   Sally's answer 5
4   Sally remembers. 9
5   Sally meets Kuril 13
6   Sally and Kuril 15
7   Sally tries getting upside down 19
8   Edward and Sally go to meet Kuril and
    Marama 23
9   Sally and her mum talk 25
10 Sally baby sits 27
11 The day at the beach .31
12 Kuril wins the sandcastle competition 35
About the Author. 39

ACKNOWLEDGEMENTS

Many thanks to:

Erena Trenerry for her advice with the initial story, & friendship

Tracy Lieberman for proof reading, guidance & friendship

1

WHERE IT ALL BEGAN

Sally was born in Beerwah, in beautiful Queensland Australia. Growing up she was always ready to explore and often got into mischief. She liked to explore around near her home meeting many of the other animals who also lived in Beerwah.

These are some of her friends; Edward the emu, Willy the wombat, Big Red and Mary the kangaroos. As she grew older she explored more and more. Then she met Clarence the kookaburra, Dizzy the ostrich, Humpy the Camel and Kuril the water rat and his wife Marama, which began a friendship as well as wonderful and interesting adventures.

This is about two of those adventures that included all her friends.

2

THE NICKNAME

It was another hot steamy day in Beerwah and the next snack time was later that afternoon.

Sleepy Sally elephant was leaning against a tree and wondering if she should have a nap. She decided that a nap in the shade was probably a great idea, or maybe at her favourite mud hole. She really was too sleepy to care and began to wander over to the shade near her mud hole.

Just then she heard someone call her name, "Sally, Sally", Sally turned and saw Edward the emu running toward her. Ho - hum she sighed and tried to ignore him, but he kept coming and was soon standing alongside her.

He seemed excited about something and it was

obvious he wanted to talk. Sally turned to him, wishing he would go away, and in her sleepy voice asked what he was so excited about. Now Edward had a bit of a stutter and it was worse when he was excited so his reply almost seemed silly because of it.

He replied "I, yyyoouu, uuss, hhear tat, that, yyou haave a nickname". Now Sally had gently tried many times to help Edward speak properly, so she looked at Edward and in her kind elephant voice she said softly and gently, "Slow down, take a deep breath and let's put our lessons into practice, "Now what are you asking me?"

Edward stopped running and paused for a moment. Sally watched him take a deep breath, she thought he was trying to blow himself up like a balloon, and then he slowly began to repeat what he had just said. "I have been told that you have a nickname is that true? I, I heard it from Billy the Crocodile and he said it is the upside down elephant" He looked pleased with himself for saying it so well. Sally looked at him and in her kind soft elephant voice said "That was better, now I know what you are talking about. I know when you get excited you jumble your words and I do like to talk with you, so try to remember our lessons of slowing down and taking a deep breath before talking." Edward nodded and waited for Sally to begin. Sally said "Let's go down by the waterhole in the shade and we can talk there."

3

SALLY'S ANSWER

As they walked Sally looked like she was daydreaming and did not answer straight away. Edward became impatient and spluttered "ddid you, ddid you?" Sally still seemed to be far away deep in thought. Edward wondered what she was thinking about that kept her so quiet. They strolled along together and they finally came to the shade by the mud hole. Sally got comfortable; Edward ruffled his feathers and settled beside her. The two friends sat there in silence for a while, but Edward was impatient still wanting to know the story behind a nickname he had been told by Billy the old salty crocodile. He had heard that she was called "The upside down elephant" by many of her friends. Sally seemed to still be daydreaming, and what she was remembering was how she got the nickname. Edward knew that elephants had a long memory, a bit better than his, which seemed to only remember a few things each day, so he waited patiently for an answer. Sally was remembering how her mother had described her to a friend… "Definitely one of a kind, affectionate, cheeky and endearing beyond words, she is a delight and often reminds me of a human child, always looking for adventure and forever getting up to mischief. And Sally absolutely loves her food." Sally also remembered what her teacher wrote on her report card "Sally- a very independent elephant and always the first to try new things and to see how far she can push the boundaries. She has a strong determination; there is no mountain high enough to stop her from getting what she wants. She will go far in life".

As she lay in the shade remembering while Edward sat beside her, Sally looked at him and said "So Billy the old Salty said I was called the upside down elephant did he?" "Yes" said Edward excitedly as he waited for her to go on.

"Mmmm I wonder if he is right?" teased Sally, "Maybe he is making it up just to get you excited over nothing"

Poor Edward he did not know what to say and just sat there silently looking a little disappointed. Then Edward shook his feathers and started to move to get up, he was thinking how mean it was of old Salty to play such a trick on him. He thought to himself "I… I… I do not like a trick like that, it is mean!" Just then Sally sprayed some dust over her back and stretched out a little more. Edward said "Well I think I will wander on and not listen to old Salty's tales ever again" and he stretched up some more, ready to go. Sally seemed to wake up a bit and said "Don't go it is true I do have the nickname of the upside down elephant."

4

SALLY REMEMBERS

Edward shook his feathers and flopped down again eager and waiting to hear the story.

Sally began slowly "It all began when I was a little elephant and I loved to explore and learn about things" she paused to gather her thoughts. She was remembering the many adventures she had gotten into as she grew up. Like the time she decided to find out what was outside her home fence, she found a way to get out and saw many wondrous things in front of her. She saw old Salty Bill for the first time and stopped to chat to him, her mother called her back just in time, old Salty Bill was looking hungrily at her and thinking about how nice she would taste.

When she got a distance away from old Salty Bill she heard him laugh his crocodile laugh and he yelled out one day you will be a lovely meal for me and you won't get away, just like that elephant with the short nose. She also saw smaller animals with funny skin that looked furry and had stripes and they did not seem to want to chat, they seemed scared of her. Slowly she wandered back to her side of the fence she saw many interesting things that she wanted to explore; she promised herself that she would explore them all.

That night as she got ready to go to sleep her mother kissed her head and said "Goodnight little adventurer" Sally asked her mother what Old Salty Bill had meant about the elephant with the short nose. Her mother said "I will tell you tomorrow, now off to sleep"

So Sally went to sleep and had some wonderful dreams about exploring the sights she had seen and sounds she had heard. She dreamed she was a big as her mother and not afraid of anything. She dreamed of chatting more with Old Salty Bill but from a safe spot high on a bank while he lay on the beach below.

In her dreams she wondered about the strange animal with shiny skin and black round things for legs it had things following behind it and had humans inside it, it also made an odd rumbling noise. Was it eating the humans? You and I know it was a train to take people around so they could meet all the animals safely, but it was new and exciting for Sally. She dreamed many other dreams and woke the next morning ready for more adventures.

But right now Edward was waiting for her to tell him about the nickname and he reminded her that she had promised to tell him. So she slowly put her memories away for another time and began to tell Edward how she got her nickname.

5

SALLY MEETS KURIL

"It began one morning when I was on school holidays and I had gone out for walk, I was exploring all that was around me and watching out for that Billy the Salty croc" She said. "As I wandered around saying hi to all my animal friends I met a tiny new friend" she paused to remember him, "He was no bigger than the first part of my trunk and had a long tail and funny back feet, they reminded me of a ducks feet" Sally paused again remembering the meeting. "I looked down at this tiny animal and in my surprise to see him" she said with a laugh "I forgot I am big with a big voice, so when I spoke I saw this tiny animal put his hands over his ears and almost rolled up in ball." I said "What are you, you funny thing?"

then I remembered that my voice must have sounded like thunder to someone so small. So I tried again in a softer voice and the little animal was able to hear me this time.

He told me he was a water rat and that his name was Kuril, and proudly stated that he was an Aussie water rat. He asked me what I was and I told him I was an Asian Elephant. He looked at me again and said "A what a what a phant?" I laughed remembering to do it softly and replied "I am an Elephant"

He looked at me and walked all around me then he sat down and stared at me.

Edward was becoming impatient and said "Yes great but when did you get your nickname?" Sally sighed and realised it was a long story but did not know how to make it shorter.

She said to Edward "do you really want to know as it is a long story" Edward thought for a moment, then replied "Yes I really want to know how you became the 'Upside Down Elephant'.

Sally suggested they both get a drink of water then come back to the story. Edward sighed and said "But you often have a swim when you have a drink, then you will forget and I will miss my story" Sally kindly reminded him that elephants never forget. After they both had had a drink and Sally had sprayed water on her back and squirted some at Edward, she did it very gently so as not to knock him over, they moved back into the shade to continue the story.

6

SALLY AND KURIL

"Now where was I?" mused Sally and Edward looked at her and said "Elephants never forget" and they both laughed. Sally began again "The water rat Kuril had just wandered around me and was now sitting in front of me looking" Sally said. Kuril stared at me for a long time then said "Your weird, did you eat too much as a baby?" again he stared. Then he said "Why is your nose so long? You must need big handkerchiefs to blow it!" Sally turned to Edward and said "I was a bit surprised at this cheeky water rat" Edward replied "I would have given him the end of your trunk around his cheeky ears" Sally said "I just laughed a big elephant laugh and that made Kuril sit up and take notice.

After he uncovered his ears and could hear again" We both sat for a while just looking at each other, then I said to Kuril "I would love to be friends with you and learn about you and your family" He gave a cheeky grin and replied "I think I would love that too, but I do not think you could fit in my burrow" how we both laughed.

When I got home I told my mum about my new found friend she said "Now don't go getting into trouble with this water rat, I hear they can be mischievous" Yes Kuril and I did get into mischief but that is another story.

As Kuril and I began to learn about each other and our families we had many an adventure. Mum did meet him and soon grew to like him a little bit too.

Sally said one question kept bothering me, I wondered what the world looked like from the ground where Kuril was. Edward said "What in his burrow?" "No silly, from ground level where Kuril could see things, from that level where he lived" replied Sally.

Sally continued "I often asked Kuril what he could see and what things looked like to him". He would explain what he saw and when I lifted him on my back he was often amazed at how different life looked from my height. We both wondered how I could get to see the world from his level.

We explored with me lying down but I was still too high compared to him. We tried many things over a long time but I could never quite get the same view of life as Kuril. One day we were having an adventure along the banks of the dam near my home when I slipped and tumbled into the dam, it was more of a slide down the bank and I ended up headfirst into the dam.

Wow what fun that was, so I tried it again, I forgot Kuril was with me until I saw him sitting in the sun cleaning himself. He shouted out "Hey you nearly drowned me!, I may be a water rat but I also need to breathe" "Sorry" I said "It was such fun" as we sat in the sun and dried off we both looked at the bank and thought about what had just happened. Kuril looked at me and said

"You know if we found a dry bank and you walked down it and put your head on the ground I am sure you would see the world from where I do"

7

SALLY TRIES GETTING UPSIDE DOWN

Sally thought for a moment and Edward who was now getting excited said "Ggggoooon quicck" Sally smiled a smile of remembering then went on. I said to Kuril "Mmmm a dry bank and head down, I will give it some thought, though I must go now, so let's talk about that tomorrow"

When we met the next day Kuril had some ideas of places we could try. I had mentioned the idea to mother and she had said "Don't you dare! You could hurt yourself". But I still wanted to see the world from his level so away we went.

Down by the dam we found a bank and it seemed

dry so I gently put my front feet over the edge, then - oops I slid head first into the dam making a huge splash and wetting Kuril, other elephants came running to see what had happened. Edward laughed "I bet you all had fun" he said. We all had a good swim and sprayed lots of water around. Then Kuril and I went off to find another bank, soon the sun had dried me off and I wanted another swim, but we wanted to find the bank. We soon found another one and I tried again. This time I got both front feet comfortable going down the bank and began to slowly bring my hind legs down, using my trunk to balance me. Now I had all four feet down the bank. Then as I put my head down I started to roll forward and the next thing I knew I was in the water again, only this time I am upside down my feet waving in the air. What a splash I made. Kuril laughed and laughed.

Edward looked serious and said "did you hurt yourself?" "Only my pride" replied Sally. But now I knew I could do it I just needed to balance better. After we had dried off Kuril asked "Do you want to try again?" I hesitated but soon said yes. This time I went more slowly and rolled my trunk up a little suddenly there I was both feet on the side of the bank and my head on the ground, trunk tucked back a bit and I was able to see what it looked like at ground level. Edward said "didn't the blood run to your head and ggggive yyou a head ache?" Sally replied "Not immediately, but yes it did however I did not get a headache".

Edward looked puzzled and seemed concerned, Sally asked "What are you looking so sad about"

Edward replied "I am not sad, I am trying to figure out how you got up again" Sally laughed "Well I could have flipped over, I could have walked backward up the bank, I could have rolled over" "Well what dddid yyou do" asked Edward. "I just slowly lifted my trunk and walked forward" replied Sally.

8

EDWARD AND SALLY GO TO MEET KURIL AND MARAMA

Edward looked at Sally and said "Is that it?" Sally smiled remembering and took some time before she continued. Soon she said "Well Kuril and I went there many times and many of my friends saw me upside down and that is how I got my nickname"

Edward asked "Could I meet Kuril and see you upside down?" Sally thought for a while then she whispered "Well don't tell my mother she still does not always like Kuril and she thinks I am being stupid, even an idiot for doing it. She will not listen to my story of meeting his family and other fun things." So Edward and Sally set off, soon Kuril joined them and Sally introduced Edward to Kuril. Kuril looked at Edward's strong feathery back and asked Edward if he could ride in among those feathers. Edward agreed and Sally lifted Kuril up with her trunk, he soon snuggled in and actually fell asleep.

When they arrived at the bank Kuril woke up jumped off Edwards back and raced down to call his family. Soon there were many water rats scurrying around and Kuril introduced Edward, as Sally got upside down to talk to them all. The young rats had a great time with Edward riding on his back he would gently pick them up in his beak and put them there. Sally was in her upside down position talking to Kuril and his wife Marama. It was a wonderful afternoon.

They, all, even went for another swim in the dam with the young rats riding on Edward's back and Sally spraying the cool water in the air and gently squirting the young rats. Later Edward said "I would like ttttoooo doodddoo that again" Sally said "Slow down, breathe slowly, but yes we could and may be one day all the elephants might like to try having a picnic with the rats" Sally remembered that they must only do it in the elephant dam, otherwise Salty Bill might cause trouble. She said goodbye to Edward, Kuril and Marama and headed off to get her dinner.

9

SALLY AND HER MUM TALK

At dinner that night she told her mother about her day and the fun she had had with Edward, Kuril and Marama. As they chatted she remembered that her mother had often talked about the elephant with the short trunk. Mum asked Sally "Can you tell me about the elephant with the short trunk?"

Her mother stopped making the muffins she was cooking and began slowly "Well it happened a long time ago, and we do not know if it is true, but the story is that Old Salty the crocodile met a young elephant with a short trunk and tried to pull him into the croc pond to eat him. The young elephant pulled back and stretched his trunk and all his family now has long trunks". "Now do you have any homework or something to do?" mum asked.

Sally replied yes and went off to write a story. As she walked away she wished there was more to mums story, but it reminded her to be careful around old Salty. That night she dreamed about the day she had had and how much fun it was to be with Edward and all her friends.

Next morning as she woke to another beautiful day in Beerwah, Sally remembered it was holidays, she could look forward to more fun and adventures in the coming days. As Sally ate her breakfast she wondered what she could do today that would be exciting. Her mother reminded her to clean her room and Sally thought about how nice it would be to have someone to clean her room for her, and gave a big sigh as she went off to do what mum had told her.

Later as Sally wandered around she avoided getting too close to old Salty but was courteous and said good morning, he replied and licked his lips like he was thinking of what a tasty feed she would make.

10

SALLY BABY SITS

Sally wandered over to the tigers to say good morning and nearly trod on Willy the wombat as he trotted across the path, she jumped back in fright and Willy muttered "phew that was close" and kept trotting to do whatever wombats do. Just then Big Red, the father kangaroo hopped up and asked Sally if she would keep an eye on his Joeys while he and his wife went for a quick swim. Clarence the Kookaburra heard them talking and laughed, that upside down elephant looking after joeys ….. Ha, ha, ha, ha, ha, chuckle, chuckle. Sally and Big Red ignored him and headed off to the pasture where Mary, Big Reds wife, was waiting with the four joeys.

As Big Red and Mary headed away for a swim Sally got ready to play hide and seek, backyard cricket and many other games. Soon she was joined by Edward, Kuril, Willy wombat, Terry tiger and Clarence Kookaburra. Looking around she could see that with the joeys and the others she only needed one more to make two teams of five. Just then Dizzy the ostrich came along, they asked her if she wanted to join in a game. Very soon a great game of cricket was taking place and everyone was enjoying batting, bowling, and fielding, Clarence even took a great catch in his beak and nearly dropped it as he laughed heartily. Soon it was lunch time and Big Red and Mary were back from their swim. While Mary made lunch for all, Big Red told stories of his adventures in the outback.

Kuril listened carefully and soon had a question. "Tell me Big Red" he said "I believe from all I have heard it is very dry in the outback is that true?" Big Red replied that there is water out there but not as much as there is around here. Big Red went on to tell about Humpy the camel and many other friends he had in the outback and explained that it was nicer here in Beerwah for bringing up young joeys. Mary called everyone over for lunch and what a fun time they all had sharing sandwiches, and drinks in the shade.

Mary said it was time for the joeys afternoon nap and thanked Sally for looking after them so well. She said thank you to all the others for making the joeys morning interesting and they all waved goodbye and set off to do other things. Sally, Kuril, Edward, and Dizzy headed for Sally's spot on the bank where she could talk to Marama.

11

THE DAY AT THE BEACH

They all sat around chatting, Sally in her upside position and the others all around. Dizzy and Edward took the younger water rats for a ride on their backs and Clarence flew over to join the fun, he still found Sally's upside down position funny and had a great laugh before joining in all the chat.

It was soon time for the young water rats to have their dinner and for the others to head for their homes so all the goodbyes were said and everyone headed off. Sally, Edward, and Dizzy chatted as they went and planned what they would do the next day. Sally said Kuril had found another spot for her to stand upside down and they thought they could explore that. Dizzy said that some of Humpies relatives lived nearby and maybe they could hear more stories of the outback.

Edward was thinking, suddenly he got excited as he thought about going down the road to be near the sea and made a mess of his sentences so the others had to stop and ask him to say it slowly, because they had heard something like " lllleeessssuusgot to thhhhheeeee cccccccc"

After taking a deep breath and starting slowly Edward said "Let us go to the sea for the day." The others stopped walking and looked at Edward, "you know that sounds like a great adventure."

That night Sally dreamed of the beach, the soft sand, the waves and being there with all her friends. Next morning at breakfast her mother asked Sally to help gather some lettuces for dinner and to get some carrots as well. Sally grumbled "Mum I want to go on an adventure with my friends" Sally's mother looked at her and asked in a stern voice "What adventure is this?" "Ooh we thought we would visit some of Humpies relatives and listen to stories from the outback" Sally replied.

"And?" asked her mum. Sally couldn't stop her excitement and replied "And go to the beach" Her mum looked at her and said "The beach? Why the beach, it is nothing but sand and water. If you are thinking of the beach I had better come with you and keep an eye on you" Sally looked at her mother and replied "Mum! I am not a baby" Her mother gently looked at her and said "I know but you have never been near a beach and you do not know the problems. Now let us get the lettuce and carrots then I will come with you and we can take your friends to the beach." Sally mumbled to herself as she helped get the lettuce and carrots.

She was imagining the embarrassment of having mum along in front of her friends, as well as all her wonderful plans of playing in the sand and having a swim in the sea all being slowed down by mum. As they finished their tasks and got ready for the beach Sally's mum hummed a little elephant song to herself it had been a long time since she had visited the beach.

Sally raced ahead and gathered her friends, she warned them that her mum was tagging along, "She thinks we don't know how to look after ourselves at the beach" Sally said. Sally's mum said "I heard that, It might just be that I would like a day at the beach too" Sally jumped in fright "Mum don't sneak up on us like that!" Very soon Kuril, Marama, Clarence, Dizzy, Edward and Sally along with her Mum were headed to say a hello to Humpies friends before going to the beach.

12

KURIL WINS THE SANDCASTLE COMPETITION

The day was bright, sunny and warm as they arrived at the beach. It was a lot different to what Sally had imagined and dreamed, the surf looked very rough and instead of long white sandy beaches there were lots of sand dunes. Sally was glad her mum had come as it looked like you could easily get lost, though she did not say so. Sally also thought it would have been nice if Humpy and his friends had come along as they live in sandy areas she thought. They all played in the sand and Sally and Dizzy tried the surf. Sally managed quite well but Dizzy got knocked over and Sally had to help her up. Kuril said "The beach is interesting but I am not sure I like so much sand between my toes." Kuril also tried the surf and soon was riding waves and having a great time.

As they sat looking at the sea and wondering what to do next Sally's mum asked if anyone had ever made a sand castle. They all looked at her and said a what? So she gathered some sand and soon had a small castle made. Everyone thought it looked like fun. So they decided to see who could build the best one and Sally's mum was to be the judge. Lots of sand went flying but soon six sand castles stood proud and finished. Mother looked at each and then sat down to think about the best one. After a long time she finally said Kuril you have made the best one and Edward your one comes second. They all congratulated Kuril and Edward then everyone went into the sea for a swim before going home. Sally and her mum played life guard and made sure all were safe.

They all had a wonderful time at the beach and Edward said "I think my idea was a good one." They all cheered him for saying it so well. As they walked home past Humpy's friends they shouted out "we have been at the beach would you like to join us another time". "Hey that would be fun" the camels shouted back "let us know when you go again". At Sally's house they all said goodbye and again talked about the wonderful day they had had thanks to Edward's idea.

That night Sally dreamed of the day at the beach and her adventurous mind wondered what was over the sea and how would you get there. She dreamed of great adventures on the beach including finding somewhere in the sand dunes to get to see the beach as Kuril and family saw it. She again wondered what was over the sea. Soon she woke up and was ready to eat her breakfast then do her tasks for mum.

Soon it would another fun day with her animal friends. She especially looked forward to standing on her head and chatting with Kuril and Marama. It was fun to share her adventures with all her friends and see the world the way they saw it.

>The end
>For Now

ABOUT THE AUTHOR

Michael P. Watts is a father, grandfather, and great grandfather who loves spending time playing and daydreaming with his kids. He finds inspiration for his stories out and about in his home city of Brisbane, Queensland, Australia.

www.ingramcontent.com/pod-product-compliance
Lightning Source LLC
Chambersburg PA
CBHW021126080526
44587CB00010B/646